Stay Healthy!

What Should We Eat?

Angela Royston

Heinemann Library
Chicago, Illinois

© 2006 Heinemann Library
a division of Reed Elsevier Inc.
Chicago, Illinois

Customer Service   888–454–2279

Visit our website at www.heinemannlibrary.com

Photo research by Ruth Blair, Ginny Stroud-Lewis
Designed by Jo Hinton-Malivoire, bigtop
Printed and bound in China by South China Printing Company

10 09 08 07 06
10 9 8 7 6 5 4 3 2 1

Library of Congress Cataloging-in-Publication Data
Royston, Angela.
   What should we eat? / Angela Royston.
       p. cm. -- (Stay healthy)
   Includes bibliographical references and index.
   ISBN 1-4034-7607-1 (library binding-hardcover) -- ISBN 1-4034-7612-8
(pbk.) 1. Nutrition--Juvenile literature. I. Title. II. Series.
   RA784.R6982 2005
   613.2--dc22

                                         2005010379

Acknowledgments
The author and publisher are grateful to the following for permission to reproduce copyright material:
Alamy Images p4.(Banana Stock), 12 & 23c; Getty Images p.8 & 23b(Taxi); Harcourt Education pp.6, 10, 16, 19, 21(Gareth Boden), p.20 & 23a(Liz Eddison), pp.7, 9, 11, 13, 14, 15, 17, 22, 23d(Tudor Photography); photolibrary.com p.18; Science Photo Library p.5(Maximilian Stock Ltd).

Cover photograph of a person holding an apple reproduced with permission of Alamy. Back cover images reproduced with permission of Alamy Images (Banana Stock) and Harcourt Education (Tudor Photography).

Every effort has been made to contact copyright holders of any material reproduced in this book. Any omissions will be rectified in subsequent printings if notice is given to the publisher.

The author and publisher would like to thank Dr. Sarah Schencker, Dietitian, for her comments in the preparation of this book.

Some words are shown in bold, **like this**. You can find them in the picture glossary on page 23.

Contents

Are Some Foods Better than Others?

Your body needs many kinds of foods.

Some kinds of food are good for you, like these grapes.

But you should not eat too many
of these snacks.

Which Foods Should You Eat Most Of?

You should eat mostly vegetables, and food like rice.

Rice has lots of **starch**.

Cereal is starchy, too.

Why do you think starchy food is good for you?

Starchy food gives you **energy**.

You need energy to jump.

bread

pasta

rice

These foods are starchy, too.

You should eat some starchy
food at every meal.

Should You Eat Fruit and Vegetables?

Fruit and vegetables are good for you!

You should eat many different kinds of fruit and vegetables.

How many different kinds should you eat every day?

Count them in the picture!

Do You Need to Eat Meat?

Meat has **protein** in it.

Your body needs protein to grow.

You should eat some protein every day.

tuna fish

egg

beans

cheese

These foods have protein, too.

You do not have to eat meat to get protein.

Why Is Too Much Fat Bad for You?

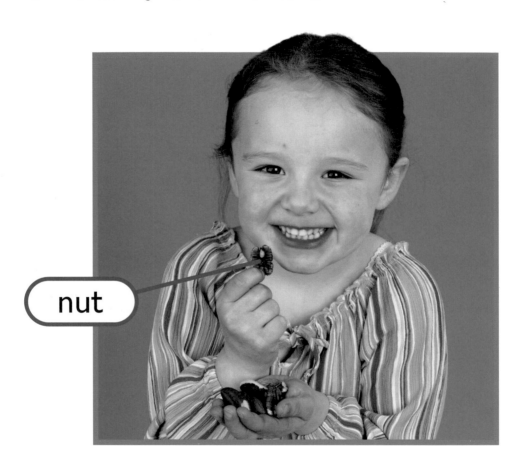

nut

You need to eat some fat.

But too much fat is bad for your heart.

ice-cream

banana

salami

Which of these snacks do you think has the least fat?

The banana has the least fat!

Are all snacks fatty?

These snacks have very little fat.

It is good to eat snacks that are low in fat.

Why Is Too Much Sugar Bad for You?

Sweet foods are tasty.

But you should have them only as treats.

Sweet foods and drinks are sugary.

Too much sugar is bad for
your teeth.

What Is a Food Allergy?

Some people are **allergic** to nuts or other foods.

They get sick if they eat these foods.

They have to make sure they do not eat these foods.

They have to check the labels on food packages.

Make a Healthy Sandwich!

1. Spread two slices of bread with butter or margarine.

2. Cover one piece of bread with the slices of cheese, tomatoes, cucumber, and lettuce.

3. Place the second slice of bread on top.

4. Enjoy eating your healthy cheese sandwich!

Glossary

 **allergic** getting sick from something that is not usually unhealthy

 **energy** power you need to move or do anything

 **protein** kind of food that helps you to grow

 **starch** food that gives you energy

Index

Note to Parents and Teachers

Reading nonfiction texts for information is an important part of a child's literacy development. Readers can be encouraged to ask simple questions and then use the text to find the answers. Most chapters in this book begin with a question. Read the questions together. Look at the pictures. Talk about what the answer might be. Then read the text to find out if your predictions were correct. To develop readers' inquiry skills, encourage them to think of other questions they might ask about the topic. Discuss where you could find the answers. Assist children in using the contents page, picture glossary, and index to practice research skills and new vocabulary.